California Real Estate Exam Prep
2024

A Complete Guide to Licensing, California-Specific Rules, Real Estate Math, and Comprehensive Practice Tests with Explanations.

By

Grant Hillwood

TABLE OF CONTENT

CHAPTER 1: INTRODUCTION TO GENERAL PRINCIPLES AND LAW

The real estate industry is governed by a complex set of principles and laws that underpin every transaction and professional relationship. These principles serve as a foundation upon which the entire industry operates. Whether you are new to the field or seeking a refresher, understanding these principles is crucial to your success in California's competitive real estate market.

Contracts

Contracts play a pivotal role in real estate, laying down the terms and obligations between parties in any transaction. A proper understanding of contracts ensures that the rights and responsibilities of all involved are clearly defined and legally protected.

Types of Real Estate Contracts

Real estate contracts vary depending on the nature of the agreement. Here are some common types:

- Purchase Agreement: Details the terms of a property's sale, including price, closing date, contingencies, and responsibilities of both parties.
- Lease Agreement: Defines the terms of a rental arrangement, such as rent amount, lease duration, and responsibilities of the landlord and tenant.
- Listing Agreement: Establishes the relationship between a seller and a real estate broker, specifying the broker's rights and obligations in selling the property.
- Option Agreement: Gives a potential buyer the right to purchase property within a specified time at an agreed price.

Essential Elements of a Contract

For a contract to be legally binding, it must contain certain essential elements:

- Offer: A proposal by one party to enter into an agreement with specific terms.
- Acceptance: The agreement by the other party to the terms of the offer.
- Consideration: Something of value exchanged between the parties, such as money or services.
- Legality of Purpose: The contract must be for a legal purpose.
- Competent Parties: Those entering into the contract must have the legal capacity to do so.
- Genuine Consent: The parties must genuinely agree to the terms without coercion, fraud, or misrepresentation.

Breach of Contract and Remedies

A breach of contract occurs when one party fails to fulfill their obligations under the agreement. This can lead to legal remedies such as:

- Damages: Financial compensation for loss suffered due to the breach.
- Specific Performance: A court order requiring the breaching party to fulfill their obligations.
- Rescission: The cancellation of the contract, with parties returning what was exchanged.

Importance in Real Estate

Contracts in real estate serve as a roadmap for transactions, providing clarity and legal safeguards. They:

- Define Relationships: Clear delineation of roles and expectations minimizes misunderstandings.
- Protect Interests: Legal terms protect parties from potential losses or unfair practices.
- Facilitate Transactions: Clearly outlined processes and responsibilities ensure smoother transactions.
- Provide Legal Recourse: In the event of disputes, contracts serve as a basis for legal resolution.

Fiduciary Duties

Fiduciary duties are obligations that an agent owes to their principal in an agency relationship. These duties form the ethical and legal foundation for real estate practice, requiring an agent to act in the best interest of their client. Understanding and fulfilling these duties is essential for maintaining trust, integrity, and professionalism in the real estate industry.

Loyalty

Loyalty requires an agent to prioritize the principal's interests above all others, including their own. This means avoiding conflicts of interest, negotiating in the principal's favor, and refraining from taking actions that could benefit the agent at the expense of the principal.

Obedience

Obedience obliges the agent to follow all lawful instructions and wishes of the principal. This involves complying with the principal's directions regarding negotiations, pricing, or other transaction-related matters, as long as those instructions do not require unlawful or unethical conduct.

Disclosure

Disclosure demands that an agent informs the principal of all relevant facts, information, and circumstances that might affect the transaction. This includes disclosing any known defects in the property, offers from other parties, or information that could influence the principal's decision-making.

Confidentiality

Confidentiality necessitates that the agent protects the principal's private information. This means not disclosing sensitive information such as motivations for buying or selling, financial details, or any other confidential information that could be used against the principal's interests.

Accounting

Accounting obliges the agent to handle the principal's money and property with the utmost care, responsibility, and transparency. This includes maintaining accurate records, handling funds in a secure and legal manner, and ensuring that all financial matters are conducted with integrity.

Reasonable Care and Diligence

Reasonable care and diligence require the agent to exercise competence, skill, and diligence in all their dealings on behalf of the principal. This means keeping up to date with market trends, performing tasks with professional competence, and taking all necessary steps to protect the principal's interests.

Potential Conflicts and Challenges

Fiduciary duties can sometimes present challenges, particularly when conflicting interests arise, such as in dual agency situations. Managing these conflicts requires careful consideration, transparency, and adherence to legal and ethical standards.

Agency Relationships

Agency relationships are central to real estate, forming the foundation for how professionals interact with clients. An agent represents the interests of a principal (such as a buyer or seller) in dealings with third parties. Understanding the intricacies of agency relationships is vital for ethical practice and legal compliance.

Types of Agency Relationships

Different types of agency relationships cater to various needs in real estate transactions:

- Seller's Agent: Represents the interests of the seller in a transaction. They are responsible for marketing the property, negotiating with buyers, and ensuring the seller's interests are protected.

- Buyer's Agent: Acts on behalf of the buyer, searching for suitable properties, negotiating with sellers, and facilitating the purchase process.
- Dual Agent: Represents both the buyer and the seller in a single transaction. This role requires careful handling to avoid conflicts of interest and to ensure that both parties' interests are represented fairly.
- Subagent: Works under another agent and represents the interests of that agent's principal. Their duties align with those of the primary agent.

Duties and Obligations

Agency relationships impose fiduciary duties, requiring the agent to act in the best interest of the principal:

- Loyalty: Always acting in the principal's best interest.
- Obedience: Following all lawful instructions from the principal.
- Disclosure: Informing the principal of all relevant facts and information.
- Confidentiality: Keeping the principal's information private and confidential.
- Accounting: Managing the principal's funds and property responsibly.
- Reasonable Care and Diligence: Providing competent and diligent services.

Creation and Termination of Agency Relationships

Agency relationships can be created through various means, such as express agreements (written or verbal), implied agreements, or estoppel (when a principal allows a third party to believe that an agency relationship exists).

Termination can occur through completion of the agency's purpose, mutual agreement, revocation by the principal, renunciation by the agent, or other legal means like death or bankruptcy of either party.

Challenges and Ethical Considerations

Navigating agency relationships can be complex, especially concerning:

- Conflicts of Interest: Particularly in dual agency, where the agent must balance the interests of two parties.
- Disclosure: Ensuring that all relevant information is shared without violating confidentiality.
- Compliance with Laws: Adhering to state and federal regulations governing agency relationships.
- Agents must approach these challenges with integrity, transparency, and a commitment to ethical practice.

CHAPTER 2: CALIFORNIA-SPECIFIC PRINCIPLES AND LAWS

California's real estate landscape is governed by a unique set of laws and regulations that distinguish it from other states. These laws affect every aspect of real estate transactions, from property rights to environmental protections and zoning ordinances. This chapter is designed to provide an in-depth look at the principles and regulations specific to California, ensuring that aspiring real estate professionals are well-versed in the state's unique legal landscape.

State Property Laws

California's state property laws are an essential framework that governs the rights, interests, and obligations of parties involved in real estate transactions. These laws cover aspects such as ownership structures, community property rules, homestead exemptions, and the protocols for title transfers. Below, we delve into these critical areas to offer readers a comprehensive understanding of California's specific property laws.

Community Property Laws

In California, community property laws stipulate that assets acquired during a marriage are considered equally owned by both spouses.

- Definition and Scope: Community property includes real estate, personal property, and income earned during the marriage. Separate property includes assets owned before the marriage or received through gifts or inheritance.
- Implications for Real Estate Transactions: Community property laws can impact sales, purchases, and refinancing decisions. For instance, both spouses must consent to sell community property, even if only one is listed on the title.
- Divorce and Death: Understanding how community property is divided in divorce or allocated upon death is vital for estate planning and family law considerations.

Homestead Exemptions

Homestead exemptions in California protect a portion of a homeowner's primary residence value from creditors.

- Eligibility and Limits: The exemption applies to primary residences and has different limits based on age, income, and other factors. As of 2024, these limits can vary widely, so real estate professionals must be aware of the current regulations.
- Filing and Enforcement: Procedures for claiming the exemption and how it protects homeowners during bankruptcy or other legal actions.

Title and Transfer Laws

These laws dictate the procedures for transferring property ownership and include critical components such as disclosures, escrow, and deeds.

- Disclosure Obligations: Sellers must disclose known defects and other material facts that could affect the property's value or desirability.
- Escrow Procedures: In California, an escrow company typically acts as a neutral third party to handle the transfer of property, ensuring all terms are met before closing.
- Deed Restrictions: Types of deeds used in California, such as grant deeds and quitclaim deeds, and their implications for transferring title.
- Transfer Taxes: Understanding the county and city transfer taxes, if applicable, can be crucial in the final transaction costs.

Environmental Regulations

California's commitment to preserving its unique and diverse environment has led to the establishment of a comprehensive set of environmental regulations. These laws impact real estate development, land use, construction, and many other aspects of the real estate industry within the state. Below, we explore some of the significant areas of environmental regulation that real estate professionals need to understand.

California Environmental Quality Act (CEQA)

CEQA is one of California's cornerstone environmental laws, designed to minimize the environmental impact of various projects, including real estate development.

- Scope and Application: CEQA applies to projects undertaken or approved by state and local public agencies. It requires an environmental review to identify potential environmental effects and ways to reduce or eliminate them.
- Environmental Impact Report (EIR): Significant projects must prepare an EIR detailing potential environmental impacts and proposing mitigation measures. The process involves public participation and can be complex and time-consuming.
- Exemptions: Certain small or less impactful projects may be exempt from CEQA requirements. Understanding these exemptions can streamline the development process.

Coastal Protection Laws

California's coastal areas are subject to specific regulations aimed at balancing development with environmental conservation.

- California Coastal Act: This act governs land use in the coastal zone, requiring permits for development and ensuring protection of coastal resources.
- Local Coastal Programs (LCPs): LCPs are developed by local governments to guide development in the coastal zone, consistent with the California Coastal Act. Real estate professionals must understand the specific LCPs governing their areas of practice.
- Public Access Requirements: Regulations may require the provision of public access to coastal areas, affecting both public and private development projects.

Hazardous Materials and Waste Regulations

The handling and disposal of hazardous materials are strictly regulated in California, affecting residential and commercial properties.

- Disclosure Requirements: Sellers and landlords must disclose the presence of certain hazardous materials, such as lead-based paint and asbestos.
- Remediation and Cleanup: Understanding the rules governing the cleanup of contaminated sites is essential for developers and property owners.

- Underground Storage Tanks: Regulations regarding the installation, maintenance, and removal of underground storage tanks can affect commercial property transactions.

Water Rights and Regulations

Water use and rights are highly regulated in California, affecting property development and use.

- Water Rights: Understanding the types of water rights, such as riparian and appropriative rights, is essential for properties near water bodies.
- Water Quality Regulations: Compliance with federal and state water quality standards impacts construction and ongoing property management.
- Floodplain Management: Properties within floodplains are subject to specific building and land-use restrictions.

Local Zoning Ordinances

Local zoning ordinances are foundational to understanding property use and development within California. These local laws govern how land can be used in different parts of a city or county and significantly impact real estate transactions, development projects, and property values. Here's an exploration of the various aspects of local zoning ordinances that real estate professionals must understand.

Zoning Categories

Local governments divide land into various zoning categories that dictate the permissible uses. These common categories include:

- Residential Zones: These regulate housing density, types of housing (e.g., single-family, multi-family), and may include restrictions on home-based businesses.
- Commercial Zones: These govern where businesses can operate and may specify types of businesses allowed.
- Industrial Zones: Designed for manufacturing and other industrial uses, with provisions for noise, emissions, and aesthetics.

- Special Purpose Zones: Including historic districts, agricultural zones, and others that require special considerations.

Land Use Controls

Zoning ordinances include specific controls that regulate how land is developed and used:

- Density Controls: These regulate the number of units or the amount of floor area on a lot, impacting housing affordability and community character.
- Height Restrictions: These determine the maximum height of buildings in a particular area.
- Setback Requirements: These specify how far buildings must be set back from property lines and can impact building design and placement.
- Parking Requirements: Regulations that define the required number of parking spaces based on the property's use.

Variance and Rezoning

Sometimes, a property owner's intended use doesn't align with existing zoning. In these cases, variances or rezoning may be pursued:

- Variances: A variance allows for an exception to a specific zoning regulation, often granted due to unique property characteristics that create hardship.
- Rezoning: This is a change in the zoning designation of a property and requires a formal process, including public hearings.

Impact on Property Transactions

Understanding local zoning ordinances is crucial for real estate professionals as they impact:

- Feasibility of Development Projects: Developers must adhere to zoning regulations, or seek variances or rezoning, which can add complexity and cost.
- Property Values: Zoning can increase or decrease property values depending on allowed uses, density, etc.

- Disclosure Obligations: Real estate professionals must be aware of zoning when representing buyers or sellers, as it may affect the buyer's intended use.

REAL ESTATE MATH ESSENTIALS

Real estate professionals require a strong understanding of various mathematical concepts that are integral to property transactions and financing. This chapter will explore the essential formulas and calculations needed for success in the real estate field. By understanding these fundamentals, readers can enhance their quantitative proficiency, essential for both the exam and real-world applications.

Mortgage Payments

Mortgage payments are a fundamental aspect of real estate transactions, encompassing the regular payments made by a borrower to a lender to repay a home loan. Understanding how to calculate and analyze mortgage payments is essential for real estate professionals, helping them guide clients in making informed decisions. This section delves into the details of mortgage payments, including the calculation of monthly payments, the understanding of amortization, and the analysis of different types of mortgage products.

Calculating Monthly Payments

The monthly mortgage payment is a fixed amount paid by the borrower to the lender, typically comprising principal, interest, taxes, and insurance (often referred to as PITI). The formula for calculating the monthly payment is:

$$M = P \times \frac{r(1+r)^n}{(1+r)^n - 1}$$

Where:

M: Monthly payment

P: Principal loan amount

r: Monthly interest rate (annual rate / 12)

n: Number of payments (loan term in years x 12)

Example

For a loan amount of $300,000 at an annual interest rate of 4% for 30 years:

- $P = \$300,000$
- $r = \frac{4\%}{12} = 0.0033$
- $n = 30 \times 12 = 360$

$$M = \$300,000 \times \frac{0.0033(1+0.0033)^{360}}{(1+0.0033)^{360}-1} \approx \$1,432.25$$

Amortization

Mortgage amortization refers to the gradual reduction of the loan balance through regular payments. An amortization schedule is a detailed breakdown of each payment into its principal and interest components.

Creating an Amortization Schedule

An amortization schedule can be created using a spreadsheet or specialized software. For each payment period, the interest is calculated on the remaining balance, and the remainder of the payment is applied to the principal.

Interest Paid: $\text{Interest} = \text{Remaining Balance} \times r$
Principal Paid: $\text{Principal} = M - \text{Interest}$
Remaining Balance: $\text{Remaining Balance} - \text{Principal}$

Repeating this process for each period will yield the complete schedule.

Mortgage Types and Payment Structures

Different types of mortgages can affect the payment structure:

- Fixed-Rate Mortgages: Payments remain constant over the life of the loan.
- Adjustable-Rate Mortgages (ARMs): Interest rates may change, affecting the monthly payment.
- Interest-Only Mortgages: Only interest is paid for a set period, resulting in lower initial payments but a remaining principal balance.

Understanding these different structures enables real estate professionals to advise clients on the best mortgage products for their needs.

Interest Calculations

Interest is a fundamental concept in real estate financing, representing the cost of borrowing money. It's typically expressed as a percentage of the principal loan amount and can be calculated in different ways depending on the loan type and terms. In this section, we will explore the various methods of calculating interest, including simple interest, compound interest, and how interest is applied in different mortgage products. Understanding these calculations is essential for real estate professionals, as they play a critical role in assessing loan affordability and advising clients on financing options.

Simple Interest

Simple interest is calculated as a percentage of the principal amount, or the initial sum of money borrowed or invested. The formula for simple interest is:

$$I = P \times r \times t$$

Where:

I: Interest

P: Principal amount

r: Annual interest rate (expressed as a decimal)

t: Time in years

Example

If you borrow $10,000 at an annual interest rate of 5% for 2 years:

$P = \$10,000$

$r = 5\% = 0.05$

$t = 2$

$$I = \$10,000 \times 0.05 \times 2 = \$1,000$$

Simple interest is used less frequently in real estate but may still be found in certain types of short-term loans.

Compound Interest

Unlike simple interest, compound interest accounts for interest on both the principal and the accumulated interest from previous periods. Compound interest can be calculated using the formula:

$$A = P \times \left(1 + \frac{r}{n}\right)^{n \times t}$$

Where:

A: Future value (including principal and interest)
P: Principal amount
r: Annual interest rate (expressed as a decimal)
n: Number of times interest is compounded per year
t: Time in years

Example

For a \$10,000 investment at an annual interest rate of 5% compounded monthly for 2 years:

$P = \$10,000$
$r = 0.05$
$n = 12$
$t = 2$

$$A = \$10,000 \times \left(1 + \frac{0.05}{12}\right)^{12 \times 2} \approx \$11,039.69$$

The interest earned is then

$$\$11,039.69 - \$10,000 = \$1,039.69.$$

Mortgage Interest

In the context of mortgages, interest is typically compounded monthly and calculated on the remaining balance of the loan. During the early stages of a fixed-rate mortgage, a higher proportion of the monthly payment goes toward interest, with more principal being paid down over time. This is reflected in the amortization schedule

Adjustable-Rate Mortgages (ARMs) may have varying interest calculations depending on the rate adjustments, which are based on specific indices.

Property Taxes

Property taxes are an essential aspect of real estate ownership and investment, constituting a significant portion of local government revenue in California. This section will guide readers through the calculation and understanding of property taxes, including assessments, exemptions, and special provisions within the state of California. Whether for a homeowner, a real estate investor, or a real estate professional, understanding property taxes is crucial for planning, budgeting, and providing accurate information to clients.

Assessment and Valuation

In California, property is assessed at its purchase price when it is bought or newly constructed. Thereafter, the property's taxable value increases by a maximum of 2% per year, unless there is a change in ownership or new construction.

The formula for the assessed value can be defined as:

$$A = P + (P \times r \times t)$$

Where:

A: Assessed value

P: Purchase price or previous year's assessed value

r: Annual increase rate (maximum of 2%, or 0.02)

t: Time in years since purchase or last assessment

Example

If a property is bought for $400,000 and assessed two years later:

$$P = \$400,000$$
$$r = 0.02$$
$$t = 2$$

$$A = \$400,000 + (\$400,000 \times 0.02 \times 2) = \$416,000$$

Calculation of Property Taxes

Once the assessed value is determined, property taxes are calculated by applying the appropriate tax rate. In California, the general property tax rate is 1% of the assessed value, plus voter-approved bonds and assessments.

$$T = A \times R + B$$

Where:

T: Total property tax

A: Assessed value

R: General tax rate (usually 1%)

B: Voter-approved bonds and assessments

Example

If the assessed value from the previous example is $416,000, and the voter-approved bonds and assessments total $3,000:

$$T = \$416,000 \times 0.01 + \$3,000 = \$7,160$$

Exemptions and Special Provisions

California offers various exemptions and special provisions that may reduce property taxes. Some of the common ones include the Homeowners' Exemption, the Disabled Veterans' Exemption, and temporary reduction in assessed value when a property suffers a decline in value.

Commissions

Commissions represent the financial rewards that real estate professionals, particularly agents and brokers, earn for their services in facilitating property transactions. Typically, these commissions are calculated as a percentage of the property's sale price. Understanding how commissions are determined, split, and distributed is vital for any aspiring real estate professional in California. This section elucidates the intricacies of commission calculations, the different structures in which they are paid, and the typical scenarios that might alter standard rates.

Basics of Commission Calculation

Commissions are usually expressed as a percentage of the sale price of a property. For example, if an agent has agreed upon a 5% commission rate with a seller, and the property sells for $500,000:

$$C = S \times r$$

Where:

C is the Commission.
S is the Sale price of the property.
r is the Commission rate.

$$C = \$500,000 \times 0.05 = \$25,000$$

Thus, the agent would earn a commission of $25,000 on that sale.

Commission Splits

Often, the commission is not kept entirely by one agent or broker. The commission may be split between:

- Listing and Selling Agents: Typically, the commission is shared between the agent representing the seller (listing agent) and the agent representing the buyer (selling agent).
- Brokerage Splits: Agents often work under brokers and are obligated to split their commission with them based on predetermined agreements.

For instance, if there's a 50-50 split between the listing and selling agent on a $25,000 commission, each agent would get $12,500. If the selling agent has a 60-40 split with their brokerage, they would keep $7,500, while their broker would get $5,000.

Variables Affecting Commission Rates

While commissions in real estate are negotiable, several factors can affect the standard rates:

- Property Type: Residential properties might have different commission percentages compared to commercial properties or raw land.
- Market Conditions: In a seller's market, with high demand and low inventory, commission rates might be lower since properties may be easier to sell. Conversely, in a buyer's market, agents might request higher commissions as selling could be more challenging.
- Agency Agreements: Some agencies might have fixed commission rates, while others might offer tiered rates based on the sale price.

Legal and Ethical Considerations

In California, it's essential to note that all commission agreements must be in writing to be enforceable. Additionally, while agents and brokers are free to negotiate their commission rates, they must always ensure that their practices don't violate any antitrust laws by setting fixed rates across the board.

Practice Exercises

The following practice exercises are designed to reinforce the concepts explained in this Chapter By working through these exercises, readers can strengthen their quantitative skills, ensuring they are well-prepared for the California real estate exam and daily real estate practice.

EXERCISE 1: COMMISSION CALCULATIONS

a. Calculate the commission for a property sold at $600,000 with a commission rate of 4%. What would be the split between the listing and selling agents if they divide it equally?

b. If the selling agent's broker takes 30% of their share, how much would the selling agent take home from that commission?

EXERCISE 2: PROPERTY TAXES

a. Calculate the annual property tax for a home assessed at $400,000, with a tax rate of 1.2%.

b. If the same property has a homestead exemption of $50,000, what would be the annual property tax?

EXERCISE 3: INTEREST CALCULATIONS

a. Calculate the monthly interest payment for a $250,000 mortgage at a 3.5% annual interest rate.

b. How much total interest would be paid over a 30-year term for the above mortgage?

EXERCISE 4: MORTGAGE PAYMENTS

a. Calculate the monthly mortgage payment for a $300,000 loan with a 4% annual interest rate and a 15-year term. Use the formula:

$$M = \frac{P \times r \times (1+r)^n}{(1+r)^n - 1}$$

Where:

M is the monthly payment.

P is the principal amount (loan amount).

r is the monthly interest rate.

n is the total number of payments.

b. How much of the first payment is applied to the principal, and how much is applied to the interest?

SOLUTIONS

Note: The answers to these exercises should be derived using the methods taught in this chapter. For complete understanding, it's recommended to solve these problems without looking at the solutions first.

Solution to 1:

a. Commission: $24,000; Listing Agent: $12,000; Selling Agent: $12,000.

b. Selling Agent's take-home: $8,400.

Solution to 2:

a. $4,800.

b. $4,200.

Solution to 3:

a. $729.17.

b. $262,500.

Solution to 4:

a. $2,219.36.

b. Principal: $664.12; Interest: $1,555.24.

These exercises should provide a robust practice session that reflects the key mathematical concepts required in the real estate field. Mastery of these topics will not only bolster the reader's exam readiness but also their competency in handling real estate transactions in California's dynamic market environment.

CHAPTER 4: GENERAL REAL ESTATE PRACTICE TESTS

The pathway to becoming a successful real estate professional isn't just about understanding the laws and regulations. It's also about understanding how to apply that knowledge in practical scenarios. The real estate world is filled with intricate scenarios that involve property valuation, finance, ethics, and much more. The best way to assess your understanding and readiness for the actual examination is through rigorous practice tests. This chapter offers a variety of these, designed to both challenge and familiarize you with the real-world applications of your studies.

Test 1: Property Valuation

1. Which method of property valuation is most commonly used to assess the value of an income-producing property?

a) Comparative Market Analysis

b) Cost Method

c) Income Capitalization Approach

d) Historical Valuation

2. The decrease in property value over time due to wear and tear is termed as:

a) Depreciation

b) Amortization

c) Deflation

d) Dissipation

3. Which principle in real estate valuation holds that the value of a specific property is influenced by the cost of acquiring an equally desirable and valuable substitute?

a) Principle of Substitution

b) Principle of Conformity

c) Principle of Contribution

d) Principle of Anticipation

4. The value of a commercial property primarily relies on which factor?

a) Aesthetics

b) Age of the property

c) Location

d) Number of bedrooms

5. In the cost approach to value, which term represents the amount that a building or other improvement adds to or subtracts from the overall property value?

a) Cost depreciation

b) Market adjustment

c) Contributory value

d) Appraisal value

6. When appraising a property using the comparative market analysis (CMA), what is most likely to be considered?

a) The original cost of the property

b) Recent sales of comparable properties

c) The future potential value

d) The property's previous appraisal value

7. Which of the following would NOT be considered in the income capitalization approach?

a) Rental income

b) Operating expenses

c) Property tax assessments

d) Depreciation

8. Which appraisal method would be most suitable for a unique property with few comparable sales, such as a historical landmark?

a) Sales comparison approach

b) Cost approach

c) Income capitalization approach

d) Gross rent multiplier

9. A new transportation hub is built near a residential neighborhood. As a result, the value of homes in the vicinity rises. This can be best explained by which principle?

a) Principle of Anticipation

b) Principle of Change

c) Principle of Competition

d) Principle of Progression

10. Which of the following best describes the principle of highest and best use?

a) The value of a property based on its potential for future development.

b) The most profitable, legally permitted, and physically possible use of a property.

c) The most common use of similar properties in a neighborhood.

d) The current use of a property and its present value.

11. External obsolescence in real estate valuation refers to:

a) Wear and tear inside a property.

b) Outdated interior design elements.

c) Loss in property value due to external factors like a new landfill nearby.

d) A decrease in property value due to structural problems.

12. What would an appraiser most likely consider when valuing a commercial property using the income capitalization approach?

a) The property's proximity to residential areas.

b) The original purchase price of the property.

c) Potential rental income and expenses.

d) The age of the property's HVAC system.

13. A property's assessed value is $300,000, and the local tax rate is 1.5%. What are the annual property taxes?

a) $3,000

b) $4,500

c) $5,000

d) $4,000

14. If a home's market value increases, but its assessed value remains the same, what will likely happen to the property's taxes?

a) Increase

b) Decrease

c) Stay the same

d) Cannot be determined

15. Which method of property valuation would be most effective for an apartment complex?

a) Sales comparison approach

b) Cost approach

c) Income capitalization approach

d) Gross rent multiplier

16. When considering the cost approach to property valuation, what is taken into account?

a) The original purchase price of the property

b) Comparable sales in the area

c) The cost to build a similar structure, minus depreciation

d) The income generated by the property

17. In a declining market, which principle explains why a higher-valued property is adversely affected by surrounding lower-valued properties?

a) Principle of Regression

b) Principle of Progression

c) Principle of Substitution

d) Principle of Contribution

18. What does the term "comparable" mean in the context of the sales comparison approach?

a) Properties with similar age, location, size, and amenities

b) Properties with similar zoning laws

c) Properties in the same neighborhood

d) Properties with the same number of rooms

19. A commercial building was sold for $800,000. If the broker's commission was 5%, what was the amount of the commission?

a) $35,000

b) $40,000

c) $45,000

d) $50,000

20. Using the Gross Rent Multiplier (GRM) method, if a property's monthly rent is $2,000 and the GRM is 150, what is the estimated value of the property?

a) $250,000

b) $300,000

c) $50,000

d) $300,000

21. The principle of substitution states that:

a) The value of a property is determined by the cost of purchasing an equivalent substitute property.

b) The value of a property increases when surrounding properties increase in value.

c) The value of a property is determined by its original purchase price.

d) The value of a property can be substituted for a tax assessment.

22. What type of valuation method is primarily used for properties that are rarely sold?

a) Sales comparison approach

b) Cost approach

c) Income capitalization approach

d) Market data method

23. In a comparative market analysis (CMA), what is considered an essential factor for choosing comparable properties?

a) The number of floors in the property

b) The price the owner originally paid

c) Recent sale prices of similar properties in the area

d) The color of the exterior

24. A property's value was appraised at $350,000. If the owner is willing to sell the property for 90% of its appraised value, what is the selling price?

a) $315,000

b) $335,000

c) $320,000

d) $310,000

24 ANSWERS TEST 1

1. c) Income Capitalization Approach: This approach is based on the return an investor would expect from the property.

2. a) Depreciation: This refers to the loss in value over time due to wear and tear.

3. a) Principle of Substitution: This principle states that a buyer will not pay more for a property than the cost of an equally desirable alternative.

4. c) Location: For commercial properties, the location is often the most critical factor in determining value.

5. c) Contributory value: This term refers to the value that a particular component (such as a building or other improvement) adds to or subtracts from the overall property value.

6. b) Recent sales of comparable properties: Comparative market analysis relies heavily on recent sales of similar properties in the area to determine the current market value.

7. d) Depreciation: While depreciation is a factor in other valuation methods, it would not typically be considered in the income capitalization approach, which is more concerned with the income a property can generate.

8. b) Cost approach: For properties with few or no comparables, like unique or historical landmarks, the cost approach (which considers the cost to reproduce the property) can provide the most accurate valuation.

9. b) Principle of Change: Real estate values are influenced by various changes in the market, such as the introduction of new infrastructure or transportation hubs.

10. b) The most profitable, legally permitted, and physically possible use of a property: This principle asserts that a property's value is maximized when its use is optimized to yield the highest return.

11. c) Loss in property value due to external factors like a new landfill nearby: External obsolescence pertains to uncontrollable external factors that can diminish a property's value.

12. c) Potential rental income and expenses: The income capitalization approach focuses on the potential income a property can generate relative to its potential expenses.

13. b) $4,500: Calculate the annual property taxes by multiplying the assessed value by the tax rate (300,000 * 0.015 = $4,500).

14. c) Stay the same: If the assessed value doesn't change, then the property taxes would remain the same regardless of the change in market value.

15. c) Income capitalization approach: This approach considers the income potential of the property, making it suitable for an apartment complex.

16. c) The cost to build a similar structure, minus depreciation: The cost approach calculates the cost to build a comparable structure and then subtracts any depreciation.

17. a) Principle of Regression: This principle explains how higher-valued properties can be negatively affected by surrounding lower-valued properties.

18. a) Properties with similar age, location, size, and amenities: In the sales comparison approach, comparables are properties with similar characteristics that have recently sold.

19. b) $40,000: The commission is calculated by multiplying the sale price by the commission rate (800,000 * 0.05 = $40,000).

20. b) $300,000: The value can be calculated by multiplying the monthly rent by the GRM (2,000 * 150 = $300,000).

21. a) The value of a property is determined by the cost of purchasing an equivalent substitute property: This principle affirms that a rational buyer wouldn't pay more for a property than the cost of an equivalent substitute.

22. b) Cost approach: This approach is often used for properties that don't frequently sell, such as unique or specialized properties.

23. c) Recent sale prices of similar properties in the area: This is the primary factor for selecting comparables in a CMA.

24. a) $315,000: The selling price is 90% of the appraised value, or (350,000 * 0.90 = $315,000).

Test 2: Real Estate Finance

1. What is the primary function of a mortgage?

a) To act as a contract between the buyer and seller

b) To serve as a legal document that describes the property

c) To secure repayment of a loan using the property as collateral

d) To record the history of the property's ownership

2. If a home buyer secures a fixed-rate mortgage at a 5% interest rate for 30 years on a $200,000 loan, what type of interest will be paid?

a) Simple Interest

b) Compound Interest

c) Annual Interest

d) Amortized Interest

3. Which type of loan allows the borrower to pay only the interest for a specific period, after which the loan must be repaid in full or converted to an amortizing loan?

a) Adjustable-Rate Mortgage (ARM)

b) Fixed-Rate Mortgage

c) Interest-Only Mortgage

d) Balloon Mortgage

4. What is a key difference between a conventional mortgage and an FHA loan?

a) FHA loans are only available to first-time homebuyers

b) Conventional mortgages always require mortgage insurance

c) FHA loans are government-insured, while conventional loans are not

d) Conventional mortgages are only available to military veterans

5. In real estate finance, what does the term "equity" refer to?

a) The total value of the property

b) The difference between the property's market value and any outstanding mortgage or other liens

c) The interest rate on the mortgage

d) The annual income generated by the property

6. A lender charges two discount points on a $300,000 loan. What is the cost of the points?

a) $3,000

b) $6,000

c) $60,000

d) $30,000

7. Which of the following best describes a subprime mortgage?

a) A mortgage for prime commercial real estate locations

b) A mortgage with an interest rate below the prime rate

c) A mortgage offered to borrowers with lower credit scores at higher interest rates

d) A mortgage offered exclusively to prime members of a financial institution

8. What does a Loan-to-Value (LTV) ratio represent in real estate finance?

a) The ratio of the loan amount to the borrower's income

b) The ratio of the loan amount to the appraised value of the property

c) The ratio of the interest rate to the loan amount

d) The ratio of the property's value to its annual rent income

9. If a borrower defaults on a mortgage, what legal process allows the lender to take possession of the property?

a) Lien

b) Foreclosure

c) Escrow

d) Easement

10. What is the main advantage of a 15-year mortgage compared to a 30-year mortgage?

a) Lower interest rates

b) Higher monthly payments

c) Larger loan amounts

d) Shorter amortization period

11. What kind of mortgage has an interest rate that changes periodically based on changes in a corresponding financial index?

a) Fixed-Rate Mortgage

b) Balloon Mortgage

c) Adjustable-Rate Mortgage (ARM)

d) Interest-Only Mortgage

12. In a real estate transaction, what does the term "closing costs" include?

a) Only the cost of the property

b) Only the lender's fees

c) The cost of repairs needed before closing

d) Various fees and expenses related to finalizing the mortgage

13. In a typical real estate transaction, what is the purpose of a Good Faith Estimate (GFE)?

a) To provide a legally binding cost of the property

b) To estimate the monthly mortgage payment

c) To provide an estimate of closing costs

d) To ensure that the borrower has good faith in the lender

14. Which type of loan is characterized by equal monthly payments that cover both interest and principal?

a) Interest-Only Loan

b) Balloon Loan

c) Fully Amortizing Loan

d) Adjustable-Rate Loan

15. What is the primary function of Fannie Mae in the real estate market?

a) To appraise properties

b) To sell commercial real estate

c) To issue mortgages directly to consumers

d) To purchase and guarantee mortgages from lenders

16. Which of the following is NOT a typical requirement for obtaining a Federal Housing Administration (FHA) loan?

a) A minimum credit score

b) A down payment of at least 3.5%

c) Private Mortgage Insurance (PMI)

d) Employment verification

17. What is a second mortgage commonly used for?

a) To purchase a second home

b) To refinance an existing mortgage

c) To tap into home equity for expenses such as home improvement

d) To replace the primary mortgage

18. If a borrower has an adjustable-rate mortgage (ARM) with a 5/1 term, what does the "5" represent?

a) The maximum number of rate adjustments

b) The interest rate for the first five years

c) The percentage of the down payment

d) The number of years with a fixed interest rate

19. What financial ratio is used by lenders to assess a borrower's ability to manage monthly housing expenses?

a) Loan-to-Value Ratio (LTV)

b) Debt-to-Income Ratio (DTI)

c) Capitalization Rate (Cap Rate)

d) Cash Flow Ratio

20. Which term refers to the right of a lender to require full repayment of a loan if the borrower defaults?

a) Foreclosure

b) Acceleration

c) Amortization

d) Appraisal

21. Which type of mortgage allows the borrower to choose from various payment options each month, including minimum payment, interest-only payment, and a fully amortizing payment?

a) Fixed-Rate Mortgage

b) Adjustable-Rate Mortgage

c) Option Adjustable-Rate Mortgage

d) Balloon Mortgage

22. A borrower is planning to purchase a $500,000 property with a 20% down payment. How much is the down payment?

a) $10,000

b) $50,000

c) $100,000

d) $200,000

23. Which loan feature allows a borrower to add new debt to the original loan amount, thereby refinancing the total into a new loan?

a) Wraparound Loan

b) Open-End Loan

c) Closed-End Loan

d) Subprime Loan

24. If an appraiser is hired to evaluate a property for loan collateral purposes, what principle will guide the appraisal process?

a) Principle of Anticipation

b) Principle of Substitution

c) Principle of Conformity

d) Principle of Change

24 ANSWERS TEST 2

1. c) To secure repayment of a loan using the property as collateral: Mortgages are used to secure the loan, allowing the lender to foreclose if payments are not made.

2. d) Amortized Interest: This type of interest is applied to fixed-rate mortgages where both principal and interest are paid over the life of the loan.

3. c) Interest-Only Mortgage: This type of mortgage allows the borrower to pay only the interest for a set period.

4. c) FHA loans are government-insured, while conventional loans are not: This is a fundamental distinction between these two loan types.

5. b) The difference between the property's market value and any outstanding mortgage or other liens: Equity represents the owner's financial interest in the property.

6. b) $6,000: Two discount points on a $300,000 loan are equivalent to 2% of the loan amount, or $6,000.

7. c) A mortgage offered to borrowers with lower credit scores at higher interest rates: Subprime mortgages cater to those with less-than-perfect credit.

8. b) The ratio of the loan amount to the appraised value of the property: LTV ratio is used by lenders to assess the risk associated with a loan.

9. b) Foreclosure: This process enables the lender to take possession of the property if the borrower defaults on the mortgage.

10. a) Lower interest rates: Generally, a shorter-term mortgage like a 15-year loan will have lower interest rates compared to a 30-year loan.

11. c) Adjustable-Rate Mortgage (ARM): The interest rate on an ARM changes periodically based on a specific financial index.

12. d) Various fees and expenses related to finalizing the mortgage: Closing costs include fees for services such as title search, appraisal, credit checks, and more.

13. c) To provide an estimate of closing costs: A GFE gives the borrower an approximation of the costs they will incur at closing.

14. c) Fully Amortizing Loan: This loan type includes equal monthly payments covering both interest and principal, leading to full repayment by the end of the term.

15. d) To purchase and guarantee mortgages from lenders: Fannie Mae operates in the secondary mortgage market, buying and guaranteeing mortgages.

16. c) Private Mortgage Insurance (PMI): FHA loans require a Mortgage Insurance Premium (MIP), not PMI.

17. c) To tap into home equity for expenses such as home improvement: Second mortgages, like home equity loans, are commonly used for such purposes.

18. d) The number of years with a fixed interest rate: In a 5/1 ARM, the interest rate is fixed for the first five years and then adjusts annually.

19. b) Debt-to-Income Ratio (DTI): DTI measures a borrower's monthly debt payments relative to their gross monthly income.

20. b) Acceleration: This term refers to the lender's right to demand the entire outstanding balance of a loan if the borrower defaults.

21. c) Option Adjustable-Rate Mortgage: This type of mortgage provides different payment options that a borrower can choose from each month.

22. c) $100,000: 20% of $500,000 is $100,000.

23. b) Open-End Loan: An open-end loan allows the borrower to add new debt to the original loan amount.

24. b) Principle of Substitution: This principle asserts that a buyer will not pay more for a property than what they would pay for an equally desirable substitute.

Test 3: Ethics in Real estate

1. What principle requires a real estate agent to put the client's interests above all others, including the agent's own interests?

a) Loyalty

b) Disclosure

c) Confidentiality

d) Obedience

2. If an agent represents both the buyer and the seller in the same transaction, this is known as:

a) Dual Agency

b) Single Agency

c) Subagency

d) Designated Agency

3. The fiduciary duties of a real estate agent do NOT include:

a) Loyalty

b) Disclosure

c) Compensation

d) Confidentiality

4. Under the Fair Housing Act, which of the following is NOT a protected class?

a) Age

b) Race

c) Religion

d) National Origin

5. When is it acceptable for a real estate agent to disclose confidential information about a client?

a) When the other party asks for it

b) At a social event

c) When required by law

d) Never

6. A real estate agent who misrepresents a property's condition to make a sale may be guilty of:

a) Fraud

b) Puffery

c) Misdirection

d) A standard practice

7. If a real estate agent is offered a gift by a third party in exchange for a client referral, what should the agent do?

a) Accept the gift

b) Reject the gift

c) Report the gift to the authorities

d) Accept the gift and share it with the client

8. What is the main purpose of the Code of Ethics established by the National Association of Realtors (NAR)?

a) To set marketing standards

b) To protect the public

c) To outline best dress practices

d) To promote competition between agents

9. In real estate, what does the term "redlining" refer to?

a) Drawing property boundaries

b) Discriminating in lending practices based on location

c) Using red ink to highlight important terms in a contract

d) Designating priority areas for development

10. A seller instructs their agent not to show the property to buyers from a certain ethnic background. What should the agent do?

a) Follow the seller's instructions

b) Ignore the seller's instructions without telling them

c) Explain to the seller that the request violates Fair Housing laws and refuse to comply

d) Ask the broker for advice

10 ANSWERS TEST 3

1. a) Loyalty

2. a) Dual Agency

3. c) Compensation

4. a) Age

5. c) When required by law

6. a) Fraud

7. b) Reject the gift

8. b) To protect the public

9. b) Discriminating in lending practices based on location

10. c) Explain to the seller that the request violates Fair Housing laws and refuse to comply

CHAPTER 5: CALIFORNIA STATE-LEVEL PRACTICE TESTS

California is known for its unique and stringent real estate laws. The state has its own regulatory framework, which dictates how real estate agents, brokers, and property managers must operate. This chapter is designed to offer practice tests specifically tailored to California's real estate market, covering state-level regulations and practices that you must be aware of to excel in the exam and your professional career.

Test 1: California Property Laws and Regulations

1. Which California law requires full disclosure of the physical condition of a property being sold?

a) Transfer Disclosure Statement (TDS)

b) California Fair Housing Act

c) California Landlord-Tenant Law

d) California Environmental Quality Act (CEQA)

2. How long must a California broker retain transaction files?

a) 2 years

b) 3 years

c) 5 years

d) 7 years

3. What is the statutory period for adverse possession in California?

a) 3 years

b) 5 years

c) 7 years

d) 10 years

4. Under California law, which type of deed provides the greatest protection to a buyer?

a) Quitclaim Deed

b) Warranty Deed

c) Grant Deed

d) Bargain and Sale Deed

5. In California, who is responsible for paying the documentary transfer tax during a property sale?

a) Buyer

b) Seller

c) Either buyer or seller, as agreed

d) Both buyer and seller, equally

6. What act in California law requires commercial property owners to disclose the property's energy use, water consumption, and greenhouse gas emissions?

a) California Environmental Protection Act

b) California Clean Air Act

c) California Green Building Standards Code

d) California Assembly Bill 802 (AB 802)

7. What is the maximum amount that can be charged for a bounced check fee in a California residential lease?

a) $10

b) $25 for the first offense, $35 for subsequent offenses

c) $50

d) No maximum fee

8. Which of the following statements is true regarding California's homestead exemption laws?

a) Only homeowners over 65 are eligible for a homestead exemption.

b) The homestead exemption applies to all types of properties.

c) The homestead exemption protects a portion of a home's equity from creditors.

d) The homestead exemption does not exist in California.

9. What is the purpose of the California Coastal Act?

a) To regulate oil drilling off the California coast

b) To protect and enhance the coastal environment

c) To promote coastal tourism

d) To manage water resources in coastal areas

10. A California real estate agent is preparing a Comparative Market Analysis (CMA) for a residential property. Which of the following is NOT a factor they should consider?

A) The seller's desired profit margin

B) Recent sales of comparable properties

C) Current market conditions

D) The location of the property

11: A California broker enters into a listing agreement with a seller. Which of the following documents is legally required to be provided to the seller?

A) A copy of the latest tax bill

B) A disclosure regarding agency relationships

C) A copy of the previous sale contract

D) A map of the property

12: In California, what is the maximum allowable period for a lease for possession of real property?

A) 1 year

B) 5 years

C) 99 years

D) No maximum period

13: Under California law, when a residential property built before 1978 is sold, what specific disclosure must the seller provide?

A) Earthquake hazard disclosure

B) Lead-based paint disclosure

C) Energy efficiency rating

D) Flood zone disclosure

14: What is the purpose of California's Megan's Law database regarding real estate?

A) To provide environmental hazard information

B) To provide information about registered sex offenders

C) To provide property tax information

D) To provide zoning and land use information

15: What is required in California for a valid real estate contract?

A) Signature of the buyer only

B) Notarization of all parties

C) A consideration and acceptance by both parties

D) Verbal agreement by both parties

16: Under California law, how long does a buyer have to request a structural pest control inspection?

A) 2 days before closing

B) 10 days after acceptance of the offer

C) 5 days before the home inspection

D) 17 days after acceptance of the offer

17: In California, what is the primary purpose of a Preliminary Title Report?

A) To display marketing statistics

B) To show previous owners of the property

C) To reveal liens, encumbrances, and other title defects

D) To provide a full property appraisal

18: Which of the following is considered community property in California?

A) Property inherited by one spouse during marriage

B) Property acquired by one spouse before marriage

C) Property purchased by one spouse during marriage with separate funds

D) Property purchased with joint funds during marriage

19: In California, under what circumstances can a property's homestead exemption be forfeited?

A) Sale of the property

B) Renting out part of the property

C) Declaring bankruptcy

D) Failure to pay property taxes

20: What does the California Mello-Roos Community Facilities Act of 1982 allow communities to do?

A) Regulate property rent within the community

B) Establish a community association

C) Levy special taxes for community improvements

D) Restrict short-term vacation rentals

21: Which of the following is NOT a requirement for the California real estate licensing exam?

A) 18 years of age

B) Background check

C) Two years of college education

D) Completion of required pre-license education

22: What is the process in California for converting personal property into real property?

A) Annexation

B) Subordination

C) Severance

D) Predation

23: In California, who typically pays the transfer tax during a real estate transaction?

A) Buyer

B) Seller

C) Both parties equally

D) The agent

24: Under California law, how long must a real estate broker retain transaction files after closing?

A) 2 years

B) 3 years

C) 5 years

D) 7 years

25: In California, what is considered an involuntary alienation of property?

A) A gift to a relative

B) Selling to a buyer

C) Foreclosure by a lender

D) Transferring to joint ownership

26: What requirement must a California residential property built before 1978 meet during a sales transaction?

A) Energy Efficiency Certification

B) Earthquake Preparedness Certification

C) Lead-Based Paint Disclosure

D) Water Conservation Inspection

26 ANSWERS TO TEST 1

1. a) Transfer Disclosure Statement (TDS)

2. b) 3 years

3. b) 5 years

4. c) Grant Deed

5. c) Either buyer or seller, as agreed

6. d) California Assembly Bill 802 (AB 802)

7. b) $25 for the first offense, $35 for subsequent offenses

8. c) The homestead exemption protects a portion of a home's equity from creditors.

9. b) To protect and enhance the coastal environment

10. A) The seller's desired profit margin

11. B) A disclosure regarding agency relationships

12. C) 99 years

13. B) Lead-based paint disclosure

14. B) To provide information about registered sex offenders

15. C) A consideration and acceptance by both parties

16. D) 17 days after acceptance of the offer

17. C) To reveal liens, encumbrances, and other title defects

18. D) Property purchased with joint funds during marriage

19. D) Failure to pay property taxes

20. C) Levy special taxes for community improvements

21. C) Two years of college education

22. A) Annexation

23. B) Seller

24. C) 5 years

25. C) Foreclosure by a lender

26. C) Lead-Based Paint Disclosure

Test 2: Environmental Regulations and Zoning Laws in California

Question 1:

Which California law requires state and local agencies to identify the significant environmental impacts of their actions?

A) CEQA (California Environmental Quality Act)

B) CERCLA (Comprehensive Environmental Response, Compensation, and Liability Act)

C) CARB (California Air Resources Board)

D) RCRA (Resource Conservation and Recovery Act)

Question 2:

What is the primary purpose of zoning laws in California?

A) To increase property tax revenue

B) To regulate building design and aesthetics

C) To control the use and development of land

D) To protect natural resources

Question 3:

In California, a variance might be granted for which of the following reasons?

A) To allow a homeowner to violate building codes

B) To allow a change to a property that is contrary to current zoning regulations

C) To speed up the permitting process

D) To reduce property taxes

Question 4:

Which California agency is responsible for regulating hazardous waste disposal?

A) California Department of Toxic Substances Control

B) California Department of Fish and Wildlife

C) California Coastal Commission

D) California Department of Water Resources

Question 5:

What type of zoning would likely be found in a California area designated for both residential and commercial use?

A) Single-Use Zoning

B) Industrial Zoning

C) Mixed-Use Zoning

D) Agricultural Zoning

Question 6:

In California, what environmental report is often required to evaluate the potential impacts of a proposed project?

A) Environmental Impact Report (EIR)

B) Environmental Risk Analysis (ERA)

C) Environmental Protection Agreement (EPA)

D) Environmental Resource Allocation (ERA)

Question 7:

What California statute sets standards for energy efficiency in new buildings?

A) Title 24

B) Title 10

C) Title 18

D) Title 35

Question 8:

A California developer wants to build near a wetland. What governmental agency would they need to obtain a permit from?

A) California Coastal Commission

B) California Department of Water Resources

C) U.S. Army Corps of Engineers

D) Both A and C

Question 9:

Which of the following is NOT a purpose of the California Coastal Act?

A) Protecting coastal resources

B) Maximizing public access to the coast

C) Promoting commercial fishing

D) Encouraging urban sprawl

Question 10:

In California, which of the following environmental aspects must be considered in a mandatory Environmental Impact Report (EIR)?

A) Potential impact on foreign trade

B) Impact on local wildlife and habitat

C) Color scheme of the proposed buildings

D) Proposed salary range for employees

Question 11:

What is the primary goal of land-use controls in California?

A) To maximize profit for landowners

B) To maintain an orderly, compatible use of land

C) To promote tourism

D) To minimize agricultural activities

Question 12:

Under California's Sustainable Groundwater Management Act (SGMA), local agencies are required to:

A) Privatize all groundwater sources

B) Develop sustainability plans for managing groundwater basins

C) Build new dams

D) Ignore groundwater depletion in drought-prone areas

Question 13:

Which California agency is responsible for the administration and enforcement of the state's land use planning and zoning laws?

A) California Department of Housing

B) California Coastal Commission

C) Department of Real Estate

D) Office of Planning and Research

Question 14:

Under California law, a developer who wants to change the zoning designation of a property must apply for:

A) A building permit

B) A coastal permit

C) A rezone

D) An environmental impact assessment

Question 15:

The California Environmental Quality Act (CEQA) requires state and local agencies to identify and mitigate the environmental impacts of:

A) Their own projects

B) Private projects

C) Both public and private projects

D) Only out-of-state projects

Question 16:

What purpose does the California Coastal Commission serve in relation to coastal property development?

A) Approving all beachfront concessions

B) Managing wildlife migration patterns

C) Regulating development within the coastal zone

D) Designating private beach areas

Question 17:

In California, who generally has the responsibility to provide public notice of a proposed zoning change?

A) The property owner

B) The local planning department

C) The buyer of the property

D) The environmental protection agency

Question 18:

Which of the following best describes California's Local Agency Formation Commissions (LAFCOs)?

A) Organizations that promote local art and culture

B) Agencies responsible for public transportation

C) Commissions that oversee the boundary changes of cities and special districts

D) Entities that handle disputes between landlords and tenants

Question 19:

In California, which document is required to assess the potential environmental impacts of a project before it's approved?

A) Impact Fee Report

B) Environmental Impact Report (EIR)

C) Coastal Development Report

D) Zoning Compliance Certificate

Question 20:

Which law in California sets the guidelines for the management and conservation of coastal and marine ecosystems?

A) Marine Life Management Act

B) Coastal Zone Management Act

C) Ocean Protection Act

D) Coastal Conservation Act

Question 21:

A landowner in California wants to divide a parcel into several smaller lots. What is the primary legal document required for this process?

A) Subdivision Map Act Compliance

B) Zoning Variance

C) Building Permit

D) Coastal Development Permit

Question 22:

In California, what is the purpose of a Conditional Use Permit (CUP)?

A) To allow temporary use of a property

B) To permit a use that is otherwise restricted by zoning laws

C) To grant immediate occupancy of a building

D) To allow construction without zoning approval

Question 23:

Which of the following is NOT a protected element under the California Environmental Quality Act (CEQA)?

A) Cultural resources

B) Aesthetic values

C) Economic factors

D) Biological resources

Question 24:

What term refers to the minimum amount of open space required around a building, as set by California zoning laws?

A) Floor Area Ratio (FAR)

B) Setback

C) Lot Coverage

D) Open Space Quotient

24 ANSWERS TO TEST 2

1. A) CEQA (California Environmental Quality Act)

2. C) To control the use and development of land

3. B) To allow a change to a property that is contrary to current zoning regulations

4. A) California Department of Toxic Substances Control

5. C) Mixed-Use Zoning

6. A) Environmental Impact Report (EIR)

7. A) Title 24

8. D) Both A and C

9. D) Encouraging urban sprawl

10. B) Impact on local wildlife and habitat

11. B) To maintain an orderly, compatible use of land

12. B) Develop sustainability plans for managing groundwater basins

13. D) Office of Planning and Research

14. C) A rezone

15. C) Both public and private projects

16. C) Regulating development within the coastal zone

17. B) The local planning department

18. C) Commissions that oversee the boundary changes of cities and special districts

19. B) Environmental Impact Report (EIR)

20. A) Marine Life Management Act

21. A) Subdivision Map Act Compliance

22. B) To permit a use that is otherwise restricted by zoning laws

23. C) Economic factors

24. B) Setback

Test 3: California Real Estate Contracts and Transactions

Question 1:

In California, what legal document must a seller provide to disclose the physical condition of the property?

A) Transfer Disclosure Statement (TDS)

B) Preliminary Title Report

C) Purchase Agreement

D) Escrow Agreement

Question 2:

Which form of listing agreement allows multiple brokers to represent a seller in California, but only the selling broker earns a commission?

A) Open Listing

B) Exclusive Agency Listing

C) Exclusive Right to Sell Listing

D) Net Listing

Question 3:

In California real estate transactions, what is the primary purpose of an earnest money deposit?

A) To pay for the property inspection

B) To compensate the selling agent

C) To show the buyer's serious intent to purchase

D) To cover closing costs

Question 4:

Under the California Residential Purchase Agreement (RPA), what is the standard number of days for a buyer to remove contingencies?

A) 7 days

B) 17 days

C) 30 days

D) 45 days

Question 5:

Which California law requires commercial property owners to disclose energy consumption reports to prospective buyers?

A) California Solar Rights Act

B) California Environmental Quality Act (CEQA)

C) California Energy Performance Act

D) California Commercial Building Energy Reporting Act

Question 6:

In a California real estate transaction, who is primarily responsible for determining the legal sufficiency of the purchase agreement?

A) The buyer

B) The seller

C) The escrow officer

D) The attorney

Question 7:

What California law mandates that specific earthquake safety information must be provided in the sale of single-family homes?

A) California Earthquake Hazard Act

B) Seismic Safety Act

C) California Earthquake Disclosure Law

D) California Transfer Disclosure Law

Question 8:

Which clause in a California real estate contract permits a buyer to cancel the contract if unable to obtain financing within a certain period?

A) Contingency Clause

B) Financing Clause

C) Mortgage Contingency Clause

D) Loan Cancellation Clause

Question 9:

What is the deadline for providing the Preliminary Title Report to the buyer in a California residential real estate transaction?

A) 5 days after acceptance

B) 10 days after acceptance

C) 15 days after acceptance

D) 20 days after acceptance

Question 10:

Under California law, who typically pays for the owner's title insurance policy?

A) Buyer

B) Seller

C) Title company

D) Both buyer and seller

Question 11:

In California, what type of deed is commonly used in residential real estate transactions to transfer title?

A) Warranty Deed

B) Bargain and Sale Deed

C) Quitclaim Deed

D) Grant Deed

Question 12:

Which form is used in California to state the terms of a rental or lease agreement?

A) Form 100

B) Form 200

C) Form 300

D) Form 400

Question 13:

In California, what does the Real Estate Settlement Procedures Act (RESPA) require to be provided within three days of a loan application?

A) Credit Report

B) Loan Estimate

C) Mortgage Statement

D) Deed of Trust

Question 14:

Which California regulation stipulates that all marketing materials must contain the licensee's name, license number, and responsible broker identity?

A) California License Law

B) Advertising Regulations Section 2799

C) Advertising Regulations Section 10140.6

D) California Disclosure Law

Question 15:

What is the maximum allowable deposit under California law for an unfurnished residential lease?

A) Two months' rent

B) Three months' rent

C) One month's rent

D) Six weeks' rent

Question 16:

Under California law, when must a buyer receive a copy of the Homeowner's Guide to Earthquake Safety?

A) During the inspection period

B) At the time of the offer

C) Before closing escrow

D) Within 10 days of listing

Question 17:

Which provision of California law requires the disclosure of a death on the property within the last three years?

A) Death Disclosure Act

B) Property Condition Disclosure Law

C) California Civil Code § 1710.2

D) California Real Estate Disclosure Law

Question 18:

In California, how long does a buyer typically have to deposit the earnest money into escrow after the acceptance of the offer?

A) 24 hours

B) 3 days

C) 7 days

D) 10 days

Question 19:

What type of deed is commonly used in California to convey title in a standard real estate sale?

A) Warranty Deed

B) Special Warranty Deed

C) Quitclaim Deed

D) Grant Deed

Question 20:

In California, if a seller fails to provide the Transfer Disclosure Statement (TDS) before the sale, what right does the buyer have?

A) Reject the property immediately

B) Rescind the offer within three days

C) Rescind the offer within five days

D) Seek legal damages only

Question 21:

Which California law governs the responsibilities and conduct of real estate brokers and salespersons?

A) Business and Professions Code

B) California Real Estate Law

C) California Commercial Code

D) Civil Rights Act

Question 22:

Under California law, what must be included in a lease agreement for a residential property built before 1978?

A) A pet policy

B) Lead-Based Paint Disclosure

C) Energy efficiency rating

D) Smart home integration guidelines

Question 23:

How often must a California real estate broker review and sign off on a salesperson's advertising?

A) Every 30 days

B) Every 3 months

C) Every 6 months

D) Once a year

Question 24:

What document must be provided to the buyer under California law if the property is located in a Natural Hazard Disclosure (NHD) area?

A) Earthquake Preparedness Guide

B) Natural Hazard Disclosure Statement

C) Flood Zone Report

D) Wildlife Risk Report

24 ANSWERS TO TEST 3

1. A) Transfer Disclosure Statement (TDS)

2. B) Exclusive Agency Listing

3. C) To show the buyer's serious intent to purchase

4. B) 17 days

5. D) California Commercial Building Energy Reporting Act

6. D) The attorney

7. A) California Earthquake Hazard Act

8. C) Mortgage Contingency Clause

9. A) 5 days after acceptance

10. B) Seller

11. D) Grant Deed

12. D) Form 400

13. B) Loan Estimate

14. C) Advertising Regulations Section 10140.6

15. A) Two months' rent

16. C) Before closing escrow

17. C) California Civil Code § 1710.2

18. B) 3 days

19. D) Grant Deed

20. C) Rescind the offer within five days

21. A) Business and Professions Code

22. B) Lead-Based Paint Disclosure

23. D) Once a year

24. B) Natural Hazard Disclosure Statement

CHAPTER 6: ESSENTIAL TOOLS FOR SUCCESS

Introduction

The California real estate market offers a multitude of opportunities, but navigating this competitive landscape requires more than just theoretical knowledge. Success in the real estate industry depends on the development of a comprehensive skill set, encompassing effective study habits, time management, exam-taking techniques, and strategies for building a successful career. This chapter provides aspiring professionals with practical tools and strategies to excel in the California real estate market.

Effective Study Habits

Setting Clear Goals

Determining your study objectives is vital. Set specific, measurable, achievable, relevant, and time-bound (SMART) goals for your real estate education.

Creating a Study Schedule

A well-structured study schedule can make all the difference. Plan your study time, break down topics into manageable parts, and stick to the schedule.

Choosing the Right Study Material

Investing in high-quality study materials, such as textbooks and practice tests specific to California real estate, ensures that you are accessing the most relevant and up-to-date information.

Utilizing Active Learning Techniques

Incorporate methods like summarizing, questioning, and teaching others. Active learning promotes deeper understanding and retention.

Time Management

Prioritizing Your Tasks

Identify what's most important and urgent. This helps in allocating time effectively.

Breaking Down Large Tasks

Divide large tasks into smaller, achievable parts. This reduces overwhelm and increases productivity.

Utilizing Technology

Use digital tools like calendars and reminders to keep track of deadlines and appointments.

Avoiding Procrastination

Implement strategies to avoid delay, such as setting rewards for completing tasks and eliminating distractions.

Exam-taking Techniques

Understanding the Exam Format

Familiarize yourself with the California real estate exam structure, including question types and scoring methods.

Practicing with Simulated Exams

Regular practice with simulated exams can build confidence and highlight areas for improvement.

Managing Exam Anxiety

Develop techniques to handle stress, such as breathing exercises and focusing on positive outcomes.

Time Management During the Exam

Use your exam time wisely by quickly answering questions you know and marking difficult ones for review later.

Building a Successful Career in Real Estate

Networking

Build connections with other real estate professionals and attend industry events.

Continuing Education

Embrace ongoing learning by attending seminars, workshops, and pursuing additional certifications.

Developing a Personal Brand

Create a recognizable and trustworthy brand by focusing on your unique strengths and values.

Setting Long-term Career Goals

Outline your career path and set achievable milestones, adjusting as needed.

CHAPTER 7: CALIFORNIA PRACTICE EXAM SIMULATION

In this concluding chapter, we present a simulated California Practice Exam, crafted to closely mimic the actual examination's structure and content. This comprehensive practice test serves as a vital tool for you, the aspiring real estate professional, to gauge your readiness for the exam, familiarize yourself with the real exam's format, and pinpoint any areas that may require last-minute review.

Please take this test in a timed setting to simulate the real examination experience. Afterward, consult the answers and explanations provided at the end of the test to assess your performance.

General Real Estate Principles (20 Questions)

Question 1:

Which of the following best describes a freehold estate?

A) An estate for years

B) A life estate

C) A leasehold estate

D) A periodic estate

Question 2:

In California, a listing agreement between a seller and a broker must contain:

A) The seller's social security number

B) The expiration date

C) The buyer's name

D) The mortgage lender's approval

Question 3:

What is a fiduciary relationship in real estate?

A) A relationship between buyer and lender

B) A relationship between two co-brokers

C) A relationship of trust and confidence between principal and agent

D) A relationship between tenant and landlord

Question 4:

The principle that states that no two parcels of property are exactly the same is known as:

A) Substitution

B) Contribution

C) Conformity

D) Uniqueness

Question 5:

Which of the following is NOT a legal method of describing real property?

A) Metes and Bounds

B) Lot and Block

C) Street Address

D) Government Survey

Question 6:

What type of lease requires the tenant to pay property taxes, insurance, and maintenance in addition to rent?

A) Gross Lease

B) Net Lease

C) Percentage Lease

D) Sandwich Lease

Question 7:

Under California law, which of the following must a broker do with client funds?

A) Mix them with his personal funds

B) Deposit them in a non-interest bearing account

C) Deposit them in a trust account

D) Invest them in the stock market

Question 8:

A client's earnest money must be deposited into the escrow account within how many days of acceptance of an offer in California?

A) 1 day

B) 3 days

C) 5 days

D) 7 days

Question 9:

What best describes a subagent in real estate?

A) An agent who represents both buyer and seller

B) An agent who works under another agent

C) An agent who works for the seller only

D) An agent who represents the buyer only

Question 10:

A broker's duty to keep the principal informed of all the facts that could affect a transaction is known as:

A) Obedience

B) Loyalty

C) Disclosure

D) Accountability

Question 11:

A real estate agent acting under a special agency agreement has the authority to:

A) Bind the principal to any contract

B) Perform a single act on behalf of the principal

C) Manage all of the principal's financial affairs

D) Enter into multiple contracts on behalf of the principal

Question 12:

A property manager's primary fiduciary duty is to:

A) The tenants of the property

B) The owner of the property

C) The real estate brokerage firm

D) The local real estate association

Question 13:

Which clause in a mortgage allows the lender to declare the entire loan balance due if the borrower defaults?

A) Alienation clause

B) Acceleration clause

C) Defeasance clause

D) Escalation clause

Question 14:

What would typically trigger a due-on-sale clause in a mortgage?

A) Death of the borrower

B) Transfer of title without lender's consent

C) Increase in property taxes

D) Refinancing of the property

Question 15:

Which of the following describes the right of a government to take private property for public use?

A) Escheat

B) Eminent domain

C) Adverse possession

D) Encroachment

Question 16:

What kind of lease typically has a rent amount based on a percentage of the tenant's gross sales?

A) Gross Lease

B) Net Lease

C) Percentage Lease

D) Sandwich Lease

Question 17:

In California, what document must be provided to the buyer if the property is located in a natural hazard zone?

A) Title report

B) Natural Hazard Disclosure Statement

C) Lead-based paint disclosure

D) Seller's affidavit

Question 18:

Which term describes the process of converting personal property into real property?

A) Annexation

B) Severance

C) Subrogation

D) Amortization

Question 19:

What type of ownership is characterized by undivided interest with the right of survivorship?

A) Tenancy in common

B) Joint tenancy

C) Tenancy by the entirety

D) Community property

Question 20:

What is the purpose of California's Real Estate Recovery Fund?

A) To provide funds for real estate education

B) To compensate victims of fraudulent real estate practices

C) To subsidize housing for low-income families

D) To support the real estate commission's administrative expenses

ANSWERS

Question 1:

Answer: B) A life estate

Explanation: A life estate is a type of freehold estate that lasts for the life of a specified individual, typically the holder of the estate. Unlike leasehold estates, which are considered less-than-freehold, a life estate grants ownership rights for a lifetime, with certain restrictions.

Question 2:

Answer: B) The expiration date

Explanation: In California, a listing agreement between a seller and a broker must contain the expiration date. This is a legal requirement to ensure clarity regarding the termination of the agreement.

Question 3:

Answer: C) A relationship of trust and confidence between principal and agent

Explanation: A fiduciary relationship in real estate is one where there is trust and confidence between the principal (such as a buyer or seller) and the agent (such as a broker). The agent is expected to act in the principal's best interest.

Question 4:

Answer: D) Uniqueness

Explanation: The principle of Uniqueness, also known as the Principle of Individuation, states that no two parcels of property are exactly the same. Each property is unique in location and characteristics.

Question 5:

Answer: C) Street Address

Explanation: Street Address is not a legal method of describing real property for the purpose of conveyance. Legal descriptions must be precise and typically use methods such as Metes and Bounds, Lot and Block, or Government Survey.

Question 6:

Answer: B) Net Lease

Explanation: A Net Lease requires the tenant to pay property taxes, insurance, and maintenance in addition to rent. This type of lease typically favors the landlord by passing on some of the ownership costs to the tenant.

Question 7:

Answer: C) Deposit them in a trust account

Explanation: Under California law, a broker must deposit client funds in a trust account. Mixing client funds with personal funds or investing them improperly would violate legal and ethical standards.

Question 8:

Answer: B) 3 days

Explanation: In California, a client's earnest money must be deposited into the escrow account within 3 days of acceptance of an offer. This is a statutory requirement to ensure proper handling of client funds.

Question 9:

Answer: B) An agent who works under another agent

Explanation: A subagent in real estate is an agent who works under another agent, typically within a brokerage. The subagent's responsibilities are subject to the direction of the supervising agent.

Question 10:

Answer: C) Disclosure

Explanation: A broker's duty to keep the principal informed of all the facts that could affect a transaction is known as Disclosure. This duty requires the broker to provide all relevant and material information, ensuring transparency and informed decision-making.

Question 11:

Answer: B) Perform a single act on behalf of the principal

Explanation: A special agency agreement grants the agent the authority to perform a specific, single act on behalf of the principal, without binding them to any other contracts or actions.

Question 12:

Answer: B) The owner of the property

Explanation: A property manager's primary fiduciary duty is to the owner of the property. They act in the best interests of the owner, maintaining the property, and maximizing its value.

Question 13:

Answer: B) Acceleration clause

Explanation: The acceleration clause in a mortgage allows the lender to declare the entire loan balance due if the borrower defaults, accelerating the payment requirement.

Question 14:

Answer: B) Transfer of title without lender's consent

Explanation: A due-on-sale clause is typically triggered by the transfer of title without the lender's consent, requiring the entire loan balance to be paid.

Question 15:

Answer: B) Eminent domain

Explanation: Eminent domain describes the government's right to take private property for public use, provided just compensation is given to the owner.

Question 16:

Answer: C) Percentage Lease

Explanation: A Percentage Lease typically bases the rent amount on a percentage of the tenant's gross sales, commonly used in retail leasing.

Question 17:

Answer: B) Natural Hazard Disclosure Statement

Explanation: In California, if the property is located in a natural hazard zone, the Natural Hazard Disclosure Statement must be provided to the buyer.

Question 18:

Answer: A) Annexation

Explanation: Annexation is the process of converting personal property into real property by attaching it to the land.

Question 19:

Answer: B) Joint tenancy

Explanation: Joint tenancy is characterized by undivided interest with the right of survivorship, meaning that if one tenant dies, their share passes to the surviving joint tenants.

Question 20:

Answer: B) To compensate victims of fraudulent real estate practices

Explanation: California's Real Estate Recovery Fund serves to compensate victims who have suffered monetary loss due to fraudulent real estate practices by licensed real estate professionals.

California-Specific Principles and Laws (25 Questions)

Question 1:

Which California law requires property sellers to provide a comprehensive disclosure statement to buyers?

A) Transfer Disclosure Statement Law

B) Truth in Lending Act

C) Fair Housing Act

D) Megan's Law

Question 2:

In California, what is the maximum amount a broker can charge as a late fee for rent payment?

A) 3% of the monthly rent

B) 5% of the monthly rent

C) 10% of the monthly rent

D) 6% of the monthly rent

Question 3:

Which law in California requires landlords to provide a minimum of 24 hours notice before entering a tenant's property?

A) Right of Entry Law

B) Tenant Privacy Act

C) Civil Code Section 1954

D) Rental Agreement Act

Question 4:

In California, who is responsible for the payment of a private transfer fee at the time of sale?

A) Buyer

B) Seller

C) Escrow Agent

D) Broker

Question 5:

What document provides detailed information about a property's physical condition and must be provided to the buyer under California law?

A) Property Condition Disclosure

B) Transfer Disclosure Statement

C) Preliminary Title Report

D) Home Warranty Policy

Question 6:

In California, which type of deed provides the greatest protection to a buyer?

A) Quitclaim Deed

B) Warranty Deed

C) Grant Deed

D) Bargain and Sale Deed

Question 7:

What is the primary purpose of California's Real Estate Law?

A) To regulate land development

B) To protect consumers in real estate transactions

C) To govern real estate advertising

D) To enforce zoning regulations

Question 8:

What term is used to describe a real estate agent representing both buyer and seller in a transaction in California?

A) Dual Agency

B) Sub-agency

C) Buyer's Agency

D) Non-agency

Question 9:

Under California law, how long must a real estate broker retain transaction files?

A) 2 years

B) 3 years

C) 5 years

D) 7 years

Question 10:

In California, what is the required minimum amount of continuing education for a real estate license renewal?

A) 30 hours

B) 45 hours

C) 60 hours

D) 15 hours

Question 11:

Which document is legally required in California to be delivered to the buyer by the seller or seller's agent?

A) Comparative Market Analysis

B) Preliminary Title Report

C) Transfer Disclosure Statement

D) Escrow Instructions

Question 12:

What determines the property tax rate for residential properties in California?

A) Proposition 13

B) Proposition 8

C) Fair Housing Act

D) State Real Estate Commission

Question 13:

In California, what's the time limit for a buyer to bring a lawsuit against a seller for failure to disclose known material defects?

A) 1 year

B) 2 years

C) 3 years

D) 4 years

Question 14:

What California law protects consumers against unfair, deceptive, or misleading advertising?

A) Truth in Advertising Act

B) Fair Housing Act

C) Consumer Protection Act

D) Business and Professions Code Section 17500

Question 15:

In California, under what circumstances can a broker legally commingle a client's funds with their own?

A) Under no circumstances

B) With written consent from the client

C) If the amount is less than $100

D) If the broker holds a special license

Question 16:

Which entity regulates the issuance of real estate licenses in California?

A) California Real Estate Board

B) Department of Real Estate

C) Real Estate Commission

D) State Licensing Bureau

Question 17:

How long does a buyer have to rescind a contract under California's statutory right of rescission for home equity loans?

A) 24 hours

B) 3 days

C) 7 days

D) 10 days

Question 18:

What is the term for the illegal practice of directing minority homebuyers to minority-concentrated areas in California?

A) Redlining

B) Blockbusting

C) Steering

D) Gentrification

Question 19:

What's the maximum amount that can be collected from California's Real Estate Recovery Fund for a single transaction?

A) $20,000

B) $50,000

C) $100,000

D) $250,000

Question 20:

In California, a real estate licensee must provide a copy of the signed deposit receipt to the buyer within how many days?

A) 1 day

B) 3 days

C) 5 days

D) 7 days

Question 21:

Which California statute requires that all advertising materials contain the licensee's license number?

A) Real Estate License Law

B) Truth in Advertising Act

C) California Civil Code 2079

D) Business and Professions Code Section 10140.6

Question 22:

What is the main purpose of the California Coastal Act?

A) To promote coastal development

B) To protect and preserve the coastline

C) To regulate beach tourism

D) To encourage waterfront real estate investments

Question 23:

In California, how often must a licensee renew their real estate license?

A) Every year

B) Every 2 years

C) Every 4 years

D) Every 5 years

Question 24:

Which entity in California oversees the administration of common interest developments like condominiums?

A) California Department of Housing

B) California Department of Real Estate

C) California Bureau of Condominiums

D) California Department of Consumer Affairs

Question 25:

What must a real estate agent do when advertising a listed property in California that they are not the listing agent for?

A) Obtain written consent from the listing broker

B) Display their own contact information prominently

C) Include the term "For Sale by Owner"

D) Use only the pictures provided by the seller

ANSWERS

Question 1:

Answer: A) Transfer Disclosure Statement Law

Explanation: California's Transfer Disclosure Statement Law requires property sellers to provide a comprehensive disclosure statement to buyers, detailing known material defects.

Question 2:

Answer: B) 5% of the monthly rent

Explanation: In California, the maximum amount a broker can charge as a late fee for rent payment is 5% of the monthly rent.

Question 3:

Answer: C) Civil Code Section 1954

Explanation: California Civil Code Section 1954 requires landlords to provide at least 24 hours' notice before entering a tenant's property, except in emergencies.

Question 4:

Answer: B) Seller

Explanation: In California, the seller is typically responsible for the payment of a private transfer fee at the time of sale.

Question 5:

Answer: B) Transfer Disclosure Statement

Explanation: The Transfer Disclosure Statement (TDS) in California provides detailed information about a property's physical condition and must be provided to the buyer.

Question 6:

Answer: C) Grant Deed

Explanation: In California, a Grant Deed offers the greatest protection to the buyer as it includes implied warranties against undisclosed encumbrances and ensures the grantor has the right to sell the property.

Question 7:

Answer: B) To protect consumers in real estate transactions

Explanation: California's Real Estate Law is designed primarily to protect consumers in real estate transactions by regulating licensing and practices.

Question 8:

Answer: A) Dual Agency

Explanation: In California, when a real estate agent represents both the buyer and the seller in a transaction, it is referred to as a Dual Agency.

Question 9:

Answer: B) 3 years

Explanation: Under California law, a real estate broker must retain transaction files for 3 years.

Question 10:

Answer: B) 45 hours

Explanation: In California, the required minimum amount of continuing education for real estate license renewal is 45 hours.

Question 11:

Answer: C) Transfer Disclosure Statement

Explanation: In California, the seller or seller's agent must deliver a Transfer Disclosure Statement to the buyer, which discloses material information about the property.

Question 12:

Answer: A) Proposition 13

Explanation: Proposition 13, passed in 1978, sets the property tax rate for residential properties in California at 1% of the assessed value plus any voter-approved bonds and assessments.

Question 13:

Answer: B) 2 years

Explanation: In California, a buyer has 2 years to bring a lawsuit against a seller for failure to disclose known material defects.

Question 14:

Answer: D) Business and Professions Code Section 17500

Explanation: This section of the California Business and Professions Code governs against deceptive advertising practices.

Question 15:

Answer: A) Under no circumstances

Explanation: A broker is never allowed to commingle a client's funds with their own in California.

Question 16:

Answer: B) Department of Real Estate

Explanation: The California Department of Real Estate (DRE) is responsible for regulating the issuance of real estate licenses in the state.

Question 17:

Answer: B) 3 days

Explanation: Under California's statutory right of rescission for home equity loans, a buyer has 3 days to rescind the contract.

Question 18:

Answer: C) Steering

Explanation: Steering is the practice of directing minority homebuyers to minority-concentrated areas, which is illegal in California.

Question 19:

Answer: C) $100,000

Explanation: The maximum amount that can be collected from California's Real Estate Recovery Fund for a single transaction is $100,000.

Question 20:

Answer: B) 3 days

Explanation: A real estate licensee in California must provide a copy of the signed deposit receipt to the buyer within 3 days.

Question 21:

Answer: D) Business and Professions Code Section 10140.6

Explanation: This California statute mandates that all advertising materials must contain the licensee's license number.

Question 22:

Answer: B) To protect and preserve the coastline

Explanation: The California Coastal Act is intended to protect, conserve, restore, and enhance the environment of the California coastline.

Question 23:

Answer: B) Every 2 years

Explanation: Real estate licenses in California must be renewed every 2 years.

Question 24:

Answer: B) California Department of Real Estate

Explanation: The California Department of Real Estate oversees the administration of common interest developments like condominiums.

Question 25:

Answer: A) Obtain written consent from the listing broker

Explanation: In California, when advertising a listed property that they are not the listing agent for, a real estate agent must obtain written consent from the listing broker.

Real Estate Math Essentials (15 Questions)

Question 1:

A house sells for $450,000 and the broker's commission rate is 6%. What is the total commission?

A) $27,000

B) $15,000

C) $30,000

D) $25,000

Question 2:

A property is assessed at 75% of its market value. If the market value is $400,000, what is the assessed value?

A) $250,000

B) $300,000

C) $100,000

D) $350,000

Question 3:

If a property's annual net income is $50,000 and it is valued at a 10% cap rate, what is the property's value?

A) $500,000

B) $450,000

C) $600,000

D) $550,000

Question 4:

A lot measures 200 feet by 150 feet. What is the total area in acres?

A) 0.69 acres

B) 1 acre

C) 1.5 acres

D) 0.34 acres

Question 5:

A buyer takes out a 30-year mortgage at an annual interest rate of 5%. What is the monthly interest rate?

A) 0.4167%

B) 5%

C) 0.4%

D) 0.05%

Question 6:

A 15% commission on a rental contract amounts to $900. What is the total rental price?

A) $6,000

B) $5,500

C) $6,500

D) $5,000

Question 7:

A seller is offering seller financing at 7% interest on a $200,000 loan for 20 years. What is the monthly payment, not including taxes and insurance?

A) $1,545

B) $1,600

C) $1,800

D) $1,700

Question 8:

A property's monthly rent is $1,500 and the gross rent multiplier is 180. What is the property's estimated value?

A) $270,000

B) $300,000

C) $240,000

D) $280,000

Question 9:

A property has decreased in value by 15% over 5 years. If the current value is $200,000, what was the original value?

A) $240,000

B) $225,000

C) $230,000

D) $235,000

Question 10:

A home is financed with a fixed-rate mortgage at an interest rate of 4.5%. If the monthly payment is $1,013.37, what is the total amount paid over the 30-year term?

A) $364,813

B) $355,000

C) $345,200

D) $350,000

Question 11:

A seller pays closing costs of 3% on a $300,000 home. What is the total amount of closing costs?

A) $10,000

B) $9,000

C) $8,000

D) $9,500

Question 12:

A property sold for $600,000 with a down payment of 20%. What is the amount of the mortgage?

A) $480,000

B) $520,000

C) $500,000

D) $450,000

Question 13:

A building has 5 units, each with a rent of $800 per month. If one unit is vacant, what is the annual rental income?

A) $38,400

B) $48,000

C) $44,800

D) $40,000

Question 14:

If the annual property tax on a home is $3,600 and the monthly mortgage payment is $1,200, what is the monthly payment including an escrow for taxes?

A) $1,500

B) $1,300

C) $1,400

D) $1,600

Question 15:

A buyer purchases a property for $250,000 with a down payment of 10%. If the loan term is 30 years at a fixed interest rate of 3.5%, what is the monthly principal and interest payment?

A) $1,122

B) $1,065

C) $987

D) $1,200

ANSWERS

Question 1:

Answer: A) $27,000

Explanation: The commission is calculated as 6% of $450,000, which is

$450,000 \times 0.06 = 27,000$

Question 2:

Answer: B) $300,000

Explanation: 75% of $400,000 is $400,000 \times 0.75 = 300,000$

Question 3:

Answer: A) $500,000

Explanation: The property's value can be found by dividing the annual net income by the cap rate: $50,000 \div 0.10 = 500,000$

Question 4:

Answer: A) 0.69 acres

Explanation: The area in square feet is $200 \times 150 = 30,000$ square feet. Since 1 acre is equal to 43,560 square feet, the total area in acres is $30,000 \div 43,560 \approx 0.69$ acres.

Question 5:

Answer: A) 0.4167%

Explanation: The monthly interest rate is the annual interest rate divided by 12:

$5\% \div 12 \approx 0.4167\%$

Question 6:

Answer: A) $6,000

Explanation: If 15% is $900, then the total rental price is $900 \div 0.15 = 6,000$

Question 7:

Answer: A) $1,545

Explanation: This question would typically require the use of a mortgage calculator with the given loan amount, interest rate, and term. The correct answer is $1,545.

Question 8:

Answer: A) $270,000

Explanation: The property's estimated value can be found by multiplying the monthly rent by the gross rent multiplier: $1,500 \times 180 = 270,000$.

Question 9:

Answer: A) $240,000

Explanation: If the value decreased by 15%, then the original value can be found by dividing the current value by 85%: $200,000 \div 0.85 = 240,000$.

Question 10:

Answer: A) $364,813

Explanation: The total amount paid over a 30-year term at $1,013.37 per month is

$1,013.37 \times 12 \times 30 = 364,813$

Question 11:

Answer: B) $9,000

Explanation: 3% of $300,000 is $300,000 \times 0.03 = 9,000$

Question 12:

Answer: A) $480,000

Explanation: A 20% down payment on $600,000 is $120,000, so the amount of the mortgage is $600,000 - 120,000 = 480,000$.

Question 13:

Answer: C) $44,800

Explanation: With one vacant unit, the rent from four units is $800 \times 4 = 3,200$ per month. The annual rental income is $3,200 \times 12 = 44,800$.

Question 14:

Answer: C) $1,400

Explanation: The monthly property tax is 3,600÷12=300, so the total monthly payment including the escrow for taxes is 1,200+300=1,400.

Question 15:

Answer: B) $1,065

Explanation: This question would typically require the use of a mortgage calculator with the given principal, interest rate, and loan term. The correct answer is $1,065.

California State-Level Practice (40 Questions)

Question 1:

Which of the following entities regulates real estate brokers and salespersons in California?

A) California Department of Housing

B) California Real Estate Commission

C) California Department of Real Estate

D) California Housing Authority

Question 2:

In California, what is the required pre-license education for a salesperson applicant?

A) 30 hours

B) 60 hours

C) 135 hours

D) 90 hours

Question 3:

What California law aims to prevent discrimination in housing based on race, color, religion, sex, sexual orientation, marital status, national origin, ancestry, familial status, or disability?

A) California Equal Housing Act

B) California Fair Employment and Housing Act

C) California Civil Rights Act

D) California Community Reinvestment Act

Question 4:

How many members serve on the California Real Estate Advisory Commission?

A) 5 members

B) 10 members

C) 15 members

D) 7 members

Question 5:

What type of license must a real estate professional in California have to sell businesses?

A) Business Broker License

B) Real Estate Salesperson License

C) Commercial Real Estate License

D) General Business License

Question 6:

What minimum net worth must a California real estate broker maintain if he/she handles client trust funds?

A) $5,000

B) $15,000

C) $25,000

D) $10,000

Question 7:

How many days does a California broker have to deposit trust funds into a trust account?

A) 1 business day

B) 3 business days

C) 7 calendar days

D) 5 business days

Question 8:

Under California law, how long must a real estate broker keep records of all transactions?

A) 2 years

B) 3 years

C) 5 years

D) 7 years

Question 9:

What is the minimum age requirement to apply for a real estate salesperson license in California?

A) 18 years

B) 21 years

C) 16 years

D) 20 years

Question 10:

In California, what kind of agency relationship is created when a seller signs a listing agreement with a broker?

A) General Agency

B) Special Agency

C) Dual Agency

D) No Agency

Question 11:

What is the maximum penalty for a first-time violation of unlicensed real estate activity in California?

A) $5,000 fine

B) $10,000 fine

C) $20,000 fine

D) $1,000 fine

Question 12:

In California, what is the term used to describe an offer that has been accepted but not yet fulfilled?

A) Executed Contract

B) Unilateral Contract

C) Executory Contract

D) Bilateral Contract

Question 13:

Under California law, how long must an employing broker keep a copy of an independent contractor agreement?

A) 2 years

B) 3 years

C) 4 years

D) 5 years

Question 14:

How often must a California real estate licensee complete ethics training?

A) Every year

B) Every two years

C) Every three years

D) Every four years

Question 15:

In California, what is required for a valid land contract?

A) Full payment upfront

B) A written agreement

C) Notarized signature

D) Buyer's credit check

Question 16:

How many units must a California property have to be considered a commercial property?

A) 4 or fewer units

B) 5 or more units

C) 2 or more units

D) 10 or more units

Question 17:

What form should be used in California to disclose the agency relationship to the buyer and seller?

A) Agency Disclosure Statement

B) Agency Relationship Agreement

C) Agency Confirmation Form

D) Agency Relationship Disclosure

Question 18:

What is the time limit for filing a complaint with the California Department of Real Estate regarding a licensee's conduct?

A) 1 year

B) 3 years

C) 5 years

D) 2 years

Question 19:

Under California law, which of the following is considered community property?

A) Property acquired during marriage using separate funds

B) Property acquired before marriage

C) Property acquired during marriage with joint funds

D) Inherited property during marriage

Question 20:

What must a California broker do if a salesperson leaves their employment?

A) Notify the Department of Real Estate within 5 days

B) Retain the salesperson's license

C) Return the salesperson's license to the Department of Real Estate

D) Both A and C

Question 21:

In California, what type of listing allows the seller to pay no commission if they sell the property themselves?

A) Exclusive Right to Sell Listing

B) Open Listing

C) Exclusive Agency Listing

D) Net Listing

Question 22:

What organization in California oversees the administration of real estate licenses?

A) California Real Estate Association

B) California Department of Housing

C) California Real Estate Commission

D) California Department of Real Estate

Question 23:

Under California law, when must a lender provide a borrower with a Loan Estimate?

A) Within 3 days of receiving the loan application

B) Within 7 days of receiving the loan application

C) Within 10 days of receiving the loan application

D) At closing

Question 24:

In California, what is the period during which a buyer can legally cancel a timeshare purchase?

A) 3 days

B) 7 days

C) 5 days

D) 10 days

Question 25:

What requirement must be met for a person to act as a real estate broker in California?

A) Must be at least 21 years old

B) Must be a California resident

C) Must have a high school diploma

D) Must have completed at least two years as a licensed salesperson

Question 26:

In California, how are real estate advertising laws enforced?

A) By the Federal Trade Commission

B) By local real estate boards

C) By the California Department of Real Estate

D) By the seller's broker

Question 27:

Which form is used in California to disclose the condition of the property to the buyer?

A) Real Property Condition Statement

B) Residential Property Disclosure Form

C) Transfer Disclosure Statement

D) Property Condition Report

Question 28:

What type of estate exists when a tenant occupies a rental property with the landlord's consent but without a current lease?

A) Estate at will

B) Estate for years

C) Periodic estate

D) Estate at sufferance

Question 29:

How many square feet are in an acre, according to California's land measurement standards?

A) 43,560 square feet

B) 40,000 square feet

C) 45,000 square feet

D) 50,000 square feet

Question 30:

In California, what is the maximum amount that may be reimbursed to a single claimant from the Recovery Account?

A) $20,000

B) $50,000

C) $25,000

D) $10,000

Question 31:

In California, which of the following is considered a material fact that must be disclosed to potential buyers?

A) Nearby school ratings

B) Seller's marital status

C) Death on the property more than three years ago

D) Past flooding issues

Question 32:

What document must be provided to a tenant in California if a property built before 1978 is being rented?

A) Transfer Disclosure Statement

B) Lead-Based Paint Disclosure

C) Asbestos Disclosure

D) Radon Disclosure

Question 33:

In California, what is the term for the legal process of removing a tenant from the premises?

A) Expulsion

B) Eviction

C) Extraction

D) Exclusion

Question 34:

Who is responsible for ordering a Notice of Completion in a construction project in California?

A) Contractor

B) Owner

C) Lender

D) Subcontractor

Question 35:

What is the maximum security deposit that can be charged for an unfurnished residential property in California?

A) Two months' rent

B) One month's rent

C) Three months' rent

D) No maximum limit

Question 36:

Under California law, how long does a homeowner have to rescind a contract with a home solicitor?

A) 24 hours

B) 3 days

C) 7 days

D) 10 days

Question 37:

Which act in California requires that all contracts be readable and understandable, using plain language?

A) The Plain Language Act

B) The Contract Clarity Act

C) The Consumer Contract Act

D) The Fair Communication Act

Question 38:

In California, what form of ownership is used by a husband and wife, providing equal ownership and the right of survivorship?

A) Joint Tenancy

B) Tenancy in Common

C) Community Property

D) Tenancy by the Entirety

Question 39:

Under California law, what type of interest does a vendee have in a property under a land contract?

A) Equitable Interest

B) Legal Interest

C) Joint Interest

D) Contingent Interest

Question 40:

In a California real estate transaction, when should the escrow holder release the funds?

A) When the buyer approves the property inspection

B) When the purchase agreement is signed

C) When all conditions of the sale have been met

D) When the seller accepts the offer

ANSWERS

Question 1: Answer - C) California Department of Real Estate

The California Department of Real Estate (DRE) is the entity responsible for licensing and regulating real estate brokers and salespersons in California.

Question 2: Answer - C) 135 hours

In California, a salesperson applicant is required to complete 135 hours of pre-license education.

Question 3: Answer - B) California Fair Employment and Housing Act

The California Fair Employment and Housing Act (FEHA) aims to prevent discrimination in housing and employment based on several protected factors, including race, color, religion, sex, sexual orientation, marital status, national origin, ancestry, familial status, or disability.

Question 4: Answer - B) 10 members

The California Real Estate Advisory Commission consists of 10 members.

Question 5: Answer - B) Real Estate Salesperson License

In California, a real estate salesperson license is required to sell businesses. A separate business broker license is not necessary.

Question 6: Answer - B) $15,000

A California real estate broker handling client trust funds must maintain a minimum net worth of $15,000.

Question 7: Answer - B) 3 business days

Under California law, a broker has 3 business days to deposit trust funds into a trust account.

Question 8: Answer - B) 3 years

A real estate broker in California must keep records of all transactions for 3 years.

Question 9: Answer - A) 18 years

The minimum age requirement to apply for a real estate salesperson license in California is 18 years.

Question 10: Answer - B) Special Agency

In California, when a seller signs a listing agreement with a broker, a special agency relationship is created. In a special agency, the agent is authorized to perform specific acts on behalf of the principal without having full control over the principal's affairs.

Question 11: Answer - A) $5,000 fine

Explanation: The maximum penalty for a first-time violation of unlicensed real estate activity in California is a fine of $5,000. This serves as a deterrent to individuals who may engage in real estate activities without proper licensing.

Question 12: Answer - C) Executory Contract

Explanation: An executory contract refers to a contract that has been accepted but not yet fulfilled. In real estate, it often refers to the time period after a purchase agreement has been signed but before closing.

Question 13: Answer - B) 3 years

Explanation: Under California law, an employing broker must keep a copy of an independent contractor agreement for a period of 3 years. This record-keeping ensures compliance and accountability within the profession.

Question 14: Answer - B) Every two years

Explanation: In California, real estate licensees are required to complete ethics training every two years. This mandatory training ensures that professionals uphold the highest standards of ethical behavior in their practice.

Question 15: Answer - B) A written agreement

Explanation: A valid land contract in California requires a written agreement. Oral agreements for the purchase of real property are generally unenforceable due to the Statute of Frauds.

Question 16: Answer - B) 5 or more units

Explanation: A commercial property in California is defined as one having 5 or more units. Properties with 4 or fewer units are generally considered residential.

Question 17: Answer - A) Agency Disclosure Statement

Explanation: In California, an Agency Disclosure Statement must be used to disclose the agency relationship to the buyer and seller, outlining the roles and responsibilities of each party.

Question 18: Answer - B) 3 years

Explanation: The time limit for filing a complaint with the California Department of Real Estate regarding a licensee's conduct is 3 years. This timeframe allows for proper investigation and resolution of potential misconduct.

Question 19: Answer - C) Property acquired during marriage with joint funds

Explanation: Under California law, community property includes property acquired during marriage with joint funds. Both spouses have an equal ownership interest in such property.

Question 20: Answer - D) Both A and C

Explanation: If a salesperson leaves their employment with a California broker, the broker must both notify the Department of Real Estate within 5 days and return the salesperson's license to the Department of Real Estate. These requirements are part of the regulatory framework to ensure proper oversight and compliance within the industry.

Question 21: Answer - C) Exclusive Agency Listing

Explanation: An Exclusive Agency Listing in California allows the seller to sell the property themselves and pay no commission. If another agent sells the property, the commission must be paid, but the seller retains the right to sell on their own without incurring a commission fee.

Question 22: Answer - D) California Department of Real Estate

Explanation: The California Department of Real Estate (DRE) is the organization responsible for the licensing and regulation of real estate professionals within the state.

Question 23: Answer - A) Within 3 days of receiving the loan application

Explanation: Under California law, lenders must provide borrowers with a Loan Estimate within 3 days of receiving the loan application. This document provides key details about the loan, such as interest rate, monthly payments, and total closing costs.

Question 24: Answer - C) 5 days

Explanation: In California, the buyer has the legal right to cancel a timeshare purchase within 5 days. This cooling-off period allows the buyer to reconsider and withdraw from the purchase without penalty.

Question 25: Answer - D) Must have completed at least two years as a licensed salesperson

Explanation: To act as a real estate broker in California, one must have completed at least two years of full-time licensed sales activity within the last five years before applying for the broker exam.

Question 26: Answer - C) By the California Department of Real Estate

Explanation: The California Department of Real Estate enforces real estate advertising laws in California. This oversight ensures that all advertising complies with legal standards and regulations.

Question 27: Answer - C) Transfer Disclosure Statement

Explanation: In California, the condition of the property is disclosed to the buyer using the Transfer Disclosure Statement (TDS). This form includes detailed information about the property's condition, including known defects and issues.

Question 28: Answer - A) Estate at will

Explanation: An estate at will exists when a tenant occupies a rental property with the landlord's consent but without a current lease. This type of agreement can be terminated by either party at any time without notice.

Question 29: Answer - A) 43,560 square feet

Explanation: An acre is a standard unit of area used in the United States, including California, and is equal to 43,560 square feet.

Question 30: Answer - B) $50,000

Explanation: In California, the maximum amount that may be reimbursed to a single claimant from the Recovery Account is $50,000. This account exists to compensate individuals who have suffered financial losses due to the fraudulent actions of a real estate licensee.

Question 31: Answer - D) Past flooding issues

Explanation: Past flooding issues are considered a material fact that must be disclosed to potential buyers in California. Material facts are those that could influence a buyer's decision to purchase. Things like nearby school ratings or a death on the property more than three years ago would not typically require disclosure.

Question 32: Answer - B) Lead-Based Paint Disclosure

Explanation: For properties built before 1978 in California, landlords must provide tenants with a Lead-Based Paint Disclosure. This is due to the risks associated with lead-based paint, which was commonly used in homes built before 1978.

Question 33: Answer - B) Eviction

Explanation: In California, the legal process of removing a tenant from the premises is known as eviction. This process is governed by specific laws and regulations to ensure fairness to both landlords and tenants.

Question 34: Answer - B) Owner

Explanation: The owner is responsible for ordering a Notice of Completion in a construction project in California. This notice formally signifies the completion of the project and may trigger the release of funds held in escrow or start the time running for filing mechanic's liens.

Question 35: Answer - A) Two months' rent

Explanation: In California, the maximum security deposit that can be charged for an unfurnished residential property is two months' rent. This is set to protect tenants from excessive upfront costs.

Question 36: Answer - B) 3 days

Explanation: Under California law, a homeowner has 3 days to rescind a contract with a home solicitor. This three-day right of rescission provides consumers with protection from high-pressure sales tactics.

Question 37: Answer - A) The Plain Language Act

Explanation: The Plain Language Act in California requires that all contracts be readable and understandable, using plain language. This ensures that consumers can more easily understand the terms of a contract, promoting fairness and transparency.

Question 38: Answer - C) Community Property

Explanation: In California, the form of ownership used by a husband and wife, providing equal ownership and the right of survivorship, is Community Property. This reflects California's status as a community property state, where most property acquired during marriage is owned equally by both spouses.

Question 39: Answer - A) Equitable Interest

Explanation: Under a land contract in California, the vendee (buyer) has an equitable interest in the property. This means the buyer has a right to obtain full ownership, provided they fulfill the obligations set out in the land contract.

Question 40: Answer - C) When all conditions of the sale have been met

Explanation: In a California real estate transaction, the escrow holder should release the funds when all conditions of the sale have been met. Escrow ensures that neither party has access to the funds until all agreed-upon conditions are satisfied, protecting both buyer and seller.

CONCLUSION

The path to success in California's real estate market has been meticulously laid out in this guide. Every chapter has been crafted to navigate the complexities of General Principles, California-specific regulations, Real Estate Math, and various practice tests, including the simulated California Practice Exam. As you stand on the threshold of this exciting career, remember to scan the QR code below to unlock exclusive bonuses: a flashcards app to reinforce your learning and a special PDF containing invaluable tips and common mistakes to avoid during exams. These resources are designed to enhance your readiness and confidence, transforming you into a competent professional ready to thrive in the Golden State's dynamic real estate market. Good luck, and may success be yours!

To get access to you bonuses scan the secure QRcode below

Made in the USA
Coppell, TX
24 May 2024

32656053R00074